First Facts

Farm

LONDON, NEW YORK,
MUNICH, MELBOURNE and DELHI

Written by Penelope Arlon
Designed by Victoria Harvey

Design development manager Helen Senior
Publishing manager Bridget Giles
Category publisher Sue Leonard
Production Rita Sinha
Production editor Marc Staples

First published in Great Britain in 2011 by
Dorling Kindersley Limited,
80 Strand, London, WC2R 0RL
Penguin Group (UK)

10 9 8 7 6 5 4 3 2 1
001-179611–August/11

A CIP catalogue record for this book
is available from the British Library.

ISBN 978-1-40536-814-8

Printed and bound in China by Leo Paper Products Ltd

Discover more at
www.dk.com

First Facts
Farm

Contents

Some farms grow plants, or crops, that can be turned into all sorts of food.

The farm

People have been farming for thousands of years. **Farms** are very **important** because they produce food for people to **eat.**

animals

Some farms raise animals, such as cows, pigs, or sheep.

6

horses

Before there were tractors, horses pulled farm machines like this plough. Animals are still used in some countries.

farmer

The farmer looks after the whole farm. He sometimes pays people to help him at busy times of the year.

7

A dairy farm

Cows are farmed for their meat or their **milk.** Cows that are used for milk are called **dairy** cows. They eat **grass** in the summer and hay in the **winter.**

cow family...

A male cow is called a bull – he has big horns. A female cow is just called a cow. A baby cow is a calf.

baby cows

Newborn calves stand up very quickly after they're born. They immediately drink milk from their mother. When they're bigger, they eat grass.

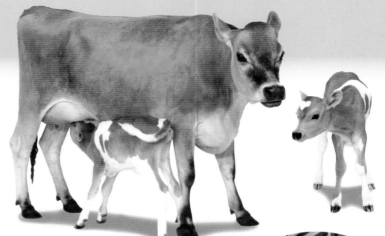

a nice drink

Milk from cows is collected for us to drink. Milk is very good for us – it keeps our bones strong.

milking cows

A cow is milked twice a day. A machine is attached to her udder and the milk flows through tubes into a big tank.

9

pig family

A male pig is called a boar, a female pig is called a sow, and baby pigs are piglets.

Pig farm

Farmers keep pigs for their meat. We use their **meat** to make sausages, ham, and bacon. Some **pigs** are pink, but others are **black** or **white** – or both.

baby piglets

Most sows have about 10 piglets at one time. A mother pig has to lie down to feed all of her babies.

pig food

Pigs are like us – they eat meat and vegetables. The farmer gives them both to keep them healthy.

pig sty

Some pigs live in fields, where they can wander around freely. Each one has its own shelter, called a sty.

11

Sheep farm

Sheep live outside all year round. They don't mind the **cold** because they have thick **woolly** coats that keep them nice and warm.

sheep family

A male sheep is called a ram. A female sheep is called a ewe, and a baby sheep is a lamb.

12

Collecting wool

In spring the sheep's fur, the fleece, is shaved, or sheared. The fleece is then turned into wool that we use to knit into socks or jumpers.

sheep dogs

To guide lots of sheep from place to place, the farmer has a sheep dog. He talks to his dog using whistles.

spring babies

In the spring the lambs are born. Sheep often give birth to twins. Young lambs are very playful.

13

Egg farm

Chickens are kept for their meat or their **eggs.** Some chickens run around outside, but **sleep** in a **hen house** at night to keep them safe from **wild** animals.

chicken family

A male chicken is called a cockerel – he shouts "cock-a-doodle-doo"! A female is called a hen, and babies are chicks.

baby chicks

A mother hen can lay up to 10 eggs. She sits on them to keep them warm until they hatch.

eggs for breakfast

The eggs we eat don't grow into chicks. The farmer pops them into boxes, and we gobble them up for breakfast!

Goose egg

Duck egg

Hen egg

other eggs

Ducks and geese also lay eggs that we can eat. Their eggs are a bit bigger than a hen's egg.

turkeys

Turkeys are huge birds that make a strange gobbbling sound.

Other farm animals

Some **big** farms keep only one type of **animal.** But smaller **farms** often have lots of different creatures **roaming** around.

alpacas

Some farmers keep alpacas, which come from South America. Their wool can be knitted into clothes.

cats

Cats are often found on farms. Farmers are happy to keep them because they catch pests like mice and rats.

goats

Goats are kept for their milk, which can be turned into delicious cheese.

horses

The farmer sometimes keeps horses for him and his family to ride. The horses live in stables.

Busy tractor

The **tractor** is the most important **vehicle** on the **farm**. It can **pull** machines that do lots of **different** jobs. A tractor's large **wheels** stop it from getting stuck in the **mud.**

grass cutter

Hay is made from grass. The tractor pulls a huge lawn mower through the field to cut the grass for drying.

baling

This tractor is pulling a baler. The baler scoops up dried grain stalks and presses them into bales.

carrying

Tractors can pull long trailers that carry heavy things. This tractor is carrying hay bales.

collecting grain

This tractor is driving next to the combine harvester. This catches the grain in the trailer it's pulling.

ploughing

The farmer uses a plough to break up the soil so he can plant seeds.

Crop farms

Some farms don't have any animals. They only grow plants for **food** for you and me. **Food** plants are called crops.

seed drill

A seed drill is pulled along the earth, dropping seeds into the soil through little pipes.

growing maize

The maize crop grows until it's ready to harvest, or pick. Then, it's delivered to our shops.

21

Harvest

When a grain **crop** needs to be cut, it's time for the combine **harvester** to start its **engine!**

cutting

The harvester's huge blades turn around and cut the stalk of the grain.

22

threshing

Inside the harvester is a big drum. It beats the crop to loosen the seeds from the top of the stalk.

unloading

The seeds are sent up a spout and poured into the back of a tractor to be taken away.

technology

Most combine harvesters have a computer on board to keep track of how much land has been cut.

23

wheat field

The seed is planted and grows into wheat. It's cut by a combine harvester.

From wheat to bread

When **wheat** has been harvested in the **combine harvester**, and the **seeds** are prepared, it can begin its journey to become **bread**.

wheat seed

The wheat is taken by tractor to a mill, where it's ground into flour.

24

flour

Sometimes the seeds are rolled around with stones to separate them from their skin. Then, they're ground into flour.

baker

The flour is taken to a baker, who mixes it with yeast and water to make into bread.

wheat foods

Wheat flour is also used to make tortillas, pasta, and breakfast cereal.

25

Other farm crops

fruit farms

When apples are ripe (ready for eating), lots of people gather together to pick the crop by hand.

Cotton picking

As well as food, farms can grow other materials like cotton. Cotton plants produce balls of fluffy fibre, which are spun into thread, then woven into fabric.

rice paddies

Rice is grown in Asia, in watery fields called paddies. The rice is the seed – white rice is the seed with the outer skin taken off.

animal bedding

After a cereal crop like wheat is harvested, the rest of the plant is cut and left to dry, so it turns into straw. Then, it's shaped into bales. Many farm animals sleep on soft straw beds.

Underground crops

Foods that grow **underground**,
like **potatoes** and carrots, need
a special **harvester**
to pick them.

harvester

The harvester
cuts off the green
parts of the plant above
ground. Then it digs
under the soil to grab
the roots, which are
good food.

carrots

The orange root of the carrot plant is the part that stores all the goodness to help the plant grow.

potatoes

The potato that we eat lies underground, and the stem and leaves grow above the ground.

onions

The onion stores the plant's goodness through winter, so it can grow again in the spring.

GRIMME

SF 1700 DLS

29

Glossary

bale
A large bundle, gathered and wrapped before it's stored or moved.

crop
A plant that's grown and harvested in large quantities, then sold.

hatch
To come out of an egg, like chicks do.

harvest
To collect or gather a crop when it's ready.

spin
To twist plant fibres like those on a cotton plant into thread or yarn to make cloth.

trailer
A big, wheeled container that's towed behind a vehicle.

udder
The large, bag-like part of a cow that holds milk for her calves.

vehicle
A machine with wheels and an engine that's used to carry people or things.

Index

Picture Credits: The publisher would like to thank the following for their kind permission to reproduce their photographs:

(Key: a-above; b-below/bottom; c-centre; f-far; l-left; r-right; t-top)

Alamy Images: Nigel Cattlin 9cr; Andrew Chittock 10tr; Ashley Cooper 18bc; Stephen Dorey ABIPP 18tc; Emil Enchev 16tr; FLPA 7b; Tim Graham 11cr; Jo Hanley 11bl; Ben Oliver 4bl, 10ca; Chris Pancewicz 20c; Diane Randell 28-29; Maurice Savage 8bl (bull); Herbie Springer 29ca; Hugh Threlfall 29tc; Edd Westmacott 10bl; WILDLIFE GmbH 11tr; Kathy Wright 13br. Corbis: Arthur Baensch 11br. Dorling Kindersley: Natural History Museum, London 15cr (goose egg); Norfolk Rural Life Museum and Union Farm 13tl; Stephen Oliver 14tr, 14bl (chick); Barrie Watts 15cr (duck egg). Dreamstime.com: Lobke Peers 15bl; Ruslanchik 15bc. Getty Images: BLOOMimage 21br; Creativ Studio Heinemann 21c, 21cr; Cultura / Colin Hawkins 7tc; Digital Vision / Creative Crop 25bl; Digital Vision / ULTRA.F 22c, 23tr; Flickr / By Kalpesh Rathod, London 27tc; Flickr / peetjohn 5tr, 24ftl; Fuse 8cb; GK Hart / Vikki Hart / Photodisc 14cl; Glow Images 25br; Iconica / Tim Platt 22-23; Nacivet / Photographer's Choice 3, 14fbl; National Geographic / Stephen St. John 19tc; Panoramic Images 21b; Photodisc / John Slater 27b, 30tr; Photodisc / Jonathan Kantor 26br; Photodisc / Lauren Nicole 26bc, 26fbr; Photodisc / Liz Whitaker 6t, 30tl; Photodisc / Paul Burns 26t; Photodisc / Sabine Scheckel 25fcl; Photodisc / Siede Preis 25tl; Photographer's Choice / Roger Spooner 27ftl, 27fcl; Photographer's Choice RF / Akira Kaede 27tr; Photographer's Choice RF / Don Farrall 4tr, 6cr, 18crb, 31tl; Photographer's Choice RF / Robin MacDougall 25cl; Photographer's Choice RF / Scott E. Barbour 13bl; Markus Renner 17tc; Riser / Bernhard Lang 5b, 24b; Stone / Brand New Images 9bl (boy); Stone / Rick Lew 8bl, 8br, 8fbl, 8fbr, 9bl, 9br, 9fbl, 9fbr. iStockphoto. com: Maria Gritcai 5cla, 18fcr (chick). Massey Ferguson / AGCO Corporation: 19b, 30br. New Holland UK Ltd: 19tl, 19c. Photolibrary: Ian Griffiths / Robert Harding Travel 19ca; Claudius Thiriet / Bios 8br (calf).

Jacket images: Front: Getty Images: GK Hart / Vikki Hart / Photodisc ftl; Image Source tr (corn). Back: Getty Images: Nacivet / Photographer's Choice fcla. Spine: Dorling Kindersley: Stephen Oliver (chick). Getty Images: f-64 Photo Office / amanaimagesRF (sunflower).

All other images © Dorling Kindersley
For further information see:
www.dkimages.com